Eulogies

CW01095854

KHAIYA A. DAI

DEDICATION

To all of those I have buried.

I don't write love poems. I write eulogies.

But all that comes out is

I Went Down to the River to Pray

I kneel and prepare to speak
to God in a big way like the
deacons and teachers at
church with grandiose poetic
language
I'm used to hearing it go on
for hours
Pleading
And sprinkled in preaching
You know
For good measure
Just in case somebody
questions the faith and
memory verses
It helps to reiterate it with
verbal gymnastics
With that in mind
I went down to the river to
pray
Not think
Or imitate my elders
Their walk is
not mine
Still no change in my gait
As I step down to the edge of
this pier

I'm ready
Bow my head
Close my eyes
Open my mouth

Love,
please don't let me ruin this

Your Stage
This is necessary
Whining
Crying
Hunch
Over
Convulsions
Dry
Heaving
A wounded creature
Screaming
And leaving flowers

Covered in shrouds
Dark in that sense

There are people who God
placed on this Earth to suffer
To mourn
The wailers

The echoes of their cries
Instruct you on how to
recognize when someone is
missing from you
Because people tend to bury
their dead too soon
And they claw their way back
through the softened insides
of pine boxes
After life
still
haunting you.

Mourners don't cry for the
living
You don't cry for the living
So give up the ghost
Floating through your mind

And let the gravity of loss
Press them
Back into the ground
Let the dead stay dead

And know that if you bury
yourself alive to follow them
No one will mourn you.

You're Too Kind
I have the tendency
to treat
everyone
with a kindness
that has proven
to be
dangerous.

Hopefully,
I will reach out to the one
who will return that kindness
and just end this
by finally
killing me

O Death
I was watching the news today
&
You know
Sometimes I've just
had it up to here with him.
He chases people who don't
even want him
and refuses to take me…
…
Imma still wait for him tho
Imma still wait

Gelus

Where are you?
I'm in the water
Face drained
Face down
Sinking
Real deep
Real low

My lungs and stomach drink
Till it hurts
And my eyes open
Searching
This night and the dirt so thick
I can't see
But I sense
This is it
Here he comes
A chill up my spine
Hairs standing on end
Warmth in my heart
Or is it burning?
And butterflies drowning in my stomach

Isn't he an absolute dream
My dream
Floats over me
And starts whispering sweet nothings
And my chest burns as I sigh
But I don't mind it

I hear his voice
"What are you doing, dear friend? Why are you in the water? "

I had to get you here

You're the only one who always comes when I call
Will you stay today?

"For me to stay I'd have to take you away
And you know that though that will happen one day, that day is not today, my friend"

I slowly lift a hand to reach for him and I sink as he shrinks away

"I love you and our visits, but I fear you've grown too accustomed to this"

A cold finger smooths my brow and I am nearly undone

"Let the water out before you drown"

No, I grow so tired of brief visits. I want this one to be our last. Take me with you.

"I cannot. But I promise to come back for you soon. Can you wait until then?"

You always come to me. But you stay just out of reach...with my Father, my friends, my hearts, why not me?
I know you want to be with me or you would not visit. You would not surround me. You would not make your presence known to me each day just to deny me the pleasure of knowing you.
Why let me come so close to you only to deny me? Why do you always leave?

"I fear..."

You lie twice now. My world knows fear. You don't.

"My affections for you will grow past my control and it is too early. I shouldn't have come in the first place. You are too young."

Youth has not stopped you before.

"But for a reason I cannot yet disclose, it gives me pause with you. Please understand."

My love for you has made me obstinate. I miss you whenever we part. I yearn for you. That's why I call out for you so. I've been trying to keep you here just one moment longer than before and another moment more so you can see how much you mean to me and I do not harbor the fear & hatred my world keeps for you. Don't you see?

I've been sinking deeper by the minute.

"My dearest friend, this is still not our time.
Please wait for me."

He knows of his power over me as he cradles me in his arms and places kisses on his hands and over me.
You know I will.

"Let this out before you drown."

He just misses my lips. kisses my cheek before
he leaves

So
I breathe
in with all the water
And cry
Watching
Through blurry eyes
As it's released

Contact High

Contact
Hiiii
Calling in the middle of the
night
Hi
Like you know I'm never
sleep
Why?
Cuz I'm thinking
Daydreaming
Drifting
Like smoke screens
Lifted
Heavy eyelids
To witness
This vision
Of the restless

Toss
And turn
Tucked into
The confines
Of my blanketed
Indecency
Around 3 in the morning
My apologies
If my musings
Make me a liability
But for the sake
Of exploring
The possibility
Of language through
Poetry in motion

Humor me

And avoid
Emotions
That make you
Feel weak

and
I know
You will
Want
Desire
Something real
Reckless
Nerve wreck
Your shit
With the sweet
Venom dripping
From my lips

Past your lips
To your lap
Up
That
Love
Line
Honey,
Under my tongue
Tied and shaken
Stirred
Senses blurred
Stuck
Now, you're talkin funny
Bite your tongue
In an attempt

To hush up the wise

Look down on me
And eat these words
Drink in the moment

When you call for it
Cuz I got you
Hi
How are you?
Real high
Hung up
On every line

Sublime
Messages
Sent to your skypager
Wait for the Drop
Of hands
Reaching towards the
Pharcyde
On a quest out
Your mind
And into mine
Trying to make sense
Of my low end theories

Elevated
Heightened
As I'm trying not
To be frightened
By the contact high

Monogamist Trust Issues

I wonder what it would be like
to be numb
normal
I hate that thought
I'd rather not
Investigate it
But I'm surrounded
by so much
 pain and hate
That I'm forced to hide myself
In order to be safe

I'm safe with you
But sometimes I think
It's because you have others

I wonder what it would be like
to have others
To not be stuck on you
To play the game
Like boys
are told to do
They fall at my feet,
but I've never taken
notice
or my rightful place on the
throne
I won't go
Without my King

The love of many sounds cool
and all
But I've seen whole nations
fall for the love of one
I've saved up all this love for
one
The second person
Who hasn't quite understood

Maybe I should
Move on
And find another
Play games with others
Be normal
I would
But
I could
I just
I only trust you

Red

Take off your clothes
And let me see

Baby please
Just a peek

At what you sneaking
Past the naked
 Eyes
For receiving
Lights
And gifted
With diamond clarity
Bright
And I see right
Through you
And reflect
On that sense
Of epiphany   .

Do you know what
Today is?
A Revelation!
Realization
Caught with your pants
Down

Overheard conversations
About gifts & dates
Texting real late
What you doing?

Reading Valentines

And single awareness
I want you to wear this
Careless
Fear of rejection
Cards & messages

Sent
Subjected
To the sweetheat
Drawn, colored &
Red
Colored in red
Why red?
Let me see
Like picture this
Chromatic filter
Focus on
Love
Read
Off my pages
And faded
Into that
Blood red
Sunset
My sights on you

Red is
The warmth
Of your presence
In a cold world

The color
Of wine
I drink
In

Punch
Drunk
Love

Red
Is carnage
& destruction
I want to tear you down
Stop
It's too much
And
It's mixed with a
Heaping teaspoon
Of lust
And chest heaving
Shallow breathing
Passion

Red is
Beautiful agony
Manifested in
Scratch marks branding
Your back
My apologies

It's the
Blood
Rushing
To meet your
Touch
To my skin

Red
Is too hot
The zone

Reminiscent of
The tone of your
Voice
Sounds so good
It has to be a sin

And I pray silently
For the Lord to have mercy
On me
 And teach me to be a lady
In the midst of this
But then again
Red is
The color of the jewelry
In the ear you've
Kissed before whispering
"You want it"

Red is
The color
Of debt
Repaid
With death
As it rushes
To our chests
And stop hearts
Shaped cards
Drawn
And colored in red
Colored in red
My words

Painting metaphysical
Portraits
As I'm the spitting image of

You deepest desires
Fondest memories
Unheard

Mindful
Of me
And colors
That you have heard
Touched
Tasted
Seen
Or recognized the scent of
That nature

Reconstruction
Paper
Making
A statement
Of love
As it
Floods our lives
and we drown in it

Sinking
Too deep
Into
A place
Where
Hallmark
Has yet
To venture

Remember

Come together

And breathe again
After that little
Death aforementioned
Float
In that suspension
Of disbelief
Afterglow
Or unity
Of timespace
Continue on
Till you see
The rose-pink
Light
Of dawn
Of the new days
Sunshine
Blinding
My eyes with
White
Surrounding
The irises I'm
Now staring into
Dilated pupils
Reminded of the truth
I'm seeking
To lay my eyes on you
Teaching
Giving new meaning
To making love

Notes
Poems
Gifts
Showing off
But sometimes

I feel like   It must be Red
None of that exists

So I address
The issue
Of hiding & disguises
When I undress you
And clothe you
In crimson robes

Adorned
With
Kisses
From the one missing from
you
This
Is
Love
In all its sweetness
That can't be purchased and
Has been done a great
Disservice

The word
Love
That is the most overused
Yet still unheard of

Simply because
To truly experience it
While completely
Naked
Blushing
And trusting

K. Michelle

Gossip spreads like fire
People breathing it
That's just unrealistic... that's
Mythical
People breathing it
Yes!
And in concentric circles no
less
To ensure I get caught in the
middle
Of it
Moving targets

Shifting focus
To the future
Blasting over club speakers
What a time to be alive
Ignis
Flies around platinum stages
Melting faces
And looking for revenge
All summer 16

Three years of searching for a
way to feel clean
Since baptism through flames
And shame
Were insufficient

Blame me
I'm left
Lukewarm and indifferent
Feeling like a D-list horror
movie with
Death trying to jump scare me
And I don't flinch anymore
Yall know Death is my nigga
and he play too damn much

Like letting You stone your
whore
With no savior to step in
To exonerate me
It's hella niggas out here with
bloody hands
And dirty feet
As a sign of accomplishment
Heart monitors still offbeat
beeping
Look who made it

Congratulations are in order
You see pillars of my rage
over your heads and mistake
them for the flames of the
Pentecost
Confusing the silence
Of my screams
For divine intervention
And He is worth praising
worth celebrating with a quip
like
God don't sleep

Love won't let me
So I hide in plain sight and
hold my breath
I know how desperately I
want(ed) to take my last
And how words could not
express how much I did not
want the defender of men to
take my first

Eventually I will surrender
Deprived of oxygen for so
long
I will burn out

I'll make sure you get wind of
it
But
I would hate to burden any of
you fire breathers with the
task of keeping track of my
ashes
So just bury me
With a closed casket
And a couple of candles from
your fake ass vigils
So I can light my way to the
next life
Where maybe
red flowers
Valentines
And I
could be cool & beautiful
again

Angel Dust
I jumped
into
love
for an angel

but his beauty
gives me pure hell
fire and
brim
stone
lit
and smoke
clears minds
as it glides
past his lips

and onto mine
possessed by
a spirit
of the sky

high
on his life
thinking I might
fall

but all
the angel wants
to do
is fly

Donte
I'm waiting for you
Now that you're out of hell
And the devil may cry
And mourn the loss of your
presence
But my own cries
for you
mixed with blood and ink
would drown that nigga out
for sure

How was it?
Fun I bet
You're not a gambling man
anymore

You got a little too lucky
before

2 30
Put your shirt on, please
the reason I'm late for class
my shirt misses yours

And the Burdens They Carry

"You tend to attract
"You tend to choose

I'm not sure
Which one sounds worse

That those who do not mean
well
Find themselves
So comfortable with me
They look for me
Or that I may be so eager to
Find them
 And never know when to
leave

I am never welcome
And I suppose I am at fault
and
I was never invited

So if I choose those who
Leave bad
And
I am not desired amongst the
good

I think that means
Something along the lines of
You are the company you
keep

Trying to play the victim here

When it was never that deep

Don't make them pull receipts
Don't
Question
When was the last time you
were healthy?

I see
A pattern
A trend, if you will
You tend to
Care too much
Without the need for
reciprocity
Supposedly

But here you are once
Again @ 2:30 in the
morning
More alone than when
you started
Crying "why me?"

Jesus Fucking Christ
You know as well as I do
That there's literally
Nobody in this room
To blame but you

And that may seem
Cold or cruel
But who gets
Mistreated
Wasted

& Rejected
more than you?

And at first
you just thought it was
Those mean kids at school
It's always been you

So get out of your God
forsaken
Broken heart & feelings
So you can decide what you
plan to do

I, for one, am tired of cleaning
up after you.

You will not recover this time,
I'll see to it

Even if it means I have
To crush you
Under the weight of that pain
So you won't move towards
Another heart again

I'll say it every day and let the
echoes of those statements
torment you @ the first
Sign of that pesky loneliness
and yearning

You are the burden
Nobody in their right mind
would take that weight

So stop trying to place it on
people
Good
Or
Bad
As you say
I want this moment to stick. I
want it to stay
Because placement
Is truly everything

Let's review
You tend to attract
You tend to choose
They never choose you
You take that pain
Take that weight
And don't. Move.

Because none of
The fuck niggas
Or real niggas
Will ever carry it for you

Vintage Glass Glitter
What is this
attention
affection
words
What type of gift is
Empty
But consciously given

What
does it take
To
Dream up
such a
thing
That wasn't real.

My consolation
Is the fire in eyes shut
sinking
And suspended in disbelief
As I'm torn to pieces.
At once I was
such a burden
But suddenly very small
Brittle
Then finally stomped out
spread out
Dazzling

What About Me?

This man I used to
Love told me
"You're only worth as much
as you make"

And for a moment
My stomach clenched
In shame at hopes
To bring him home
I made a mistake

I could see
Through my unkempt hair
And hand me down
Clothes
I was nothing

And I'm so sick
Of this constant
Battle between
Us
and them

Trying to prove to
That one percent
That we
Major
ity
bitty
Little
People like me

Who walk that

Tight rope line
Of poverty
Are trying
Not to get strung up
And hung up on it

Hang on
Move on from
Worthlessness
But remain
Aware of
It
What
However you see us

The needy
Who needs us?
For anything but
A stepping stone
Ego-boost
Helping
You feel better?

We're healers
That you secretly
Think steal your oblivious
peace
From you
In the street
With their
Incessant begging
For relief
& a place to sleep

Maybe a home

I'm hanging in there
I was going to bring you
Home
And make you wait
Outside on the
Cracked pavement
While I straightened up
Watch you wave off my
apprehension
With an
"It's okay
You have nothing to be
ashamed of"

I do
Have something
I mean
How could I ever
Share this
Broken and filthy
Building with you

The one
With whom
My experiences
Hold no value?

How could you
Cross the threshold
Into cold sitting
Rooms
 With wall presumed
To be worn away
Or eaten through
Years of living

And dying
Of laughter
And crying
Tears that seeped through the
roof
To the kitchen floor
Boards
In interesting puzzles
That I would solve
Every time
It flooded

Memories
Of trying to
Fix things
With my cousins
But tears, memories and
everything stopped flowing
When the pipes would freeze

Furnace broken
Hearts
Bleed
Choking
On bile
And
Trying to remember things
Materials
That cold tile
Kept me alive
During my trial
By self-prescribed fire

I'm tired or running from it
I do have something

I didn't think this through
I just wasn't thinking
Before I let you in
But it just needed some fixing
If I could only prove that

I do
have something
An old
Worn
Soul that is
A reflection
Of my home
And is imbued
With priceless heirloom gems
Like my weapons in Fate

How could I
Invite you
Into
My little home
When you made it
Known
That you prefer--you deserve
Mansions

Such a delusional world view
I hoped to heal
Get better with your help
Gain some more
 noticeable
Value
Wow

I thought about it

But all I know is Love
And I do
Have something
To be ashamed of

Alternatives

Instead of calling me fragile
You could have covered my
soft heart
Instead of advising me to
close and harden that heart
with thicker skin
You could have marveled at
my ability to keep it open for
you
in spite of all I've been
through

Instead of picking at me
You could have been
encouraging
That's just as fun I think
Instead of fearing my
thoughts
Your mind could have
traveled with me

Instead of pushing and
forcing me to change
You could have told stories
with your friends
about my duality
and what they have yet to see

Instead of begging and
badgering
You could have said okay
and let me sing you to sleep

Instead of trying to bury me
You could have cultivated
wonderful things
and grown with me

Instead of telling me
I was complex
You could have just requested
some assistance
and had enough patience to
figure it out

You could have met me
halfway.

Instead of saying you weren't
gentle enough
You could have tried to
smooth out your touch

But what I could have
would have
should have
just is not enough

In your stead
I am left for dead
attempting to explain
that I stayed
I prayed
I didn't walk away
because
I believed there were
alternatives.
There were alternatives.
There are alternatives.

C of JFW
This nigga

Who in undergrad wore
purple contact lenses
Like a wannabe Lelouch
Lamperouge

Wears the same ill-fitting suit
to every formal event he's
invited to

Who has nothing else in his
wardrobe outside of purple
and gold because
how else will people know
he let grown men throw mini
fridges at him
and how else will he get girls
attention

Who ain't had a retwist in a
minute

And runs a business out of his
filthy ass kitchen

Told
you
That I am not
"power couple material"
I look like a man.
I'm plain.
I need to be more feminine
And that if I don't want to
have sex it means I'm not truly
interested in you.

And you agreed.

If the reader ever met either
of you with this little bit of
context, the jokes would write
themselves.

Dear reader,
I've left you some space to do
just that. Also, drag those
people who have belittled you.
I see you. You are enough.
_____
_____
_____

Send My Regards to Your Family

See I've been sittin
I've been sittin on
Somethin for a minute
Trying to avoid labels like
#hurtbae
Bitter

But I've been meaning to let
one off in your mansions
Mans been wil'n
And can't nobody protect you

We got mad casualties on my
block
Blood on your hands
and
I'm snitchin
I'm finished
Carrying the weight of
unfounded insults and
opinions from you and yours
when they weren't with you

Hey Mom & Dad
You're welcome
For raising your son when you
wouldn't
suits for interviews for jobs he
would eventually quit because
they were beneath him
Computers
He lived with me for years
rent free
While I got my degree and he
still a 9th year student
Cleaning urine off my
bedroom floor when your

child peed himself in a
drunken stupor
Get him help for that
addiction

And Dad come here real quick
While you tell your son to use
protection when he touch me
with
my reluctant
exhausted
please leave me alone
barely consider it
consent
because of the way I chose to
get paid

You should keep in mind that
your son used the money
slipped into my G string each
night to eat each day

Speaking of my G-Strings and
Singles...

Hey Auntie
I see you still real loose
At the mouth and in life too
Bringing up a past I'm not
even ashamed of at holiday
dinners
To get over the
disappointment of
your nephew not travelling to
you
It's okay.
This past year he was free so I
hope he took the Amtrak
straight to you
I heard how much you love

trains.
Bye Auntie

Now I'm on a Megabus to
Charlotte.
The only ones I owe
apologies.
On three different occasions I
came into someone's home
and botched cooking jobs that
I could normally do in my
sleep.
I apologize
At each of those visits, I was
at a point with your grandson
Nephew
Cousin
Where my nerves were shot
and I was in so much pain
I couldn't remember my
measurements
And whether to add dry to
wet
Or how much he was gon cost
me the next week
So my sweets came out as
sour and as wrong as I felt.
I should have been better.

And you shouldn't have yelled
at me looking for him that day
in May when he chose alcohol
over his responsibilities.
You shouldn't have given him
back to me.
I even tried to put him on a
$150 plane ride so he'd make
it back on time.
There was no need to treat me

like the bad guy.
I tried.

That
Is your kin
That
Is your blood
My heart is drained enough
My spirit shattered
And unless it's to spew
ignorance and slander
Yall been silent

I'll break that
And everything you have
Everything you know
Bet you didn't
Your boy didn't tell you
But now you know
I'm a killa
You know that I'm wit it
And anyone can get it
Just like the stereotype
"women like that"
Wit ya nose turned up
I'm a villain

Showing you the monster you
half-ass raised and sent out
into the world
And you still love him because
that's your family
I understand that

But unless it's steeped in the
gratitude and apologies owed
to me
don't any of you ever in your
lives mention my name in
conversation again.

Beautiful family
Beautiful
Yall cute
Real cute
Be blessed

Op Heartbreak

Around this time last year
I was sickly
jaundice
yellow tinted
bile of spite
and envy
welling up within the depths
of my fears
and drained from my eyes
in the form of bitter tears

ripped
away at my insides
as I knew I was too old to
function
and too young to die

"why
did you
take
your love
from me"

And
abuse it
then hand it back
and tell me there's room for
improvement
while I can't move
on account of applying
pressure to
my bleeding heart
with love

freshly carved from
it
laid out right in front of you
It was a decent start
but
you still said prove it
So, you devoured it
and threw it back up
Were you disgusted?

and told me to remove it
And I tried not to lose this
"it"
this
thing
I called you
my Love
Do you miss me?
Am I missing from you?
When you were kissing her
did you think of me too?
think
and pray
maybe the day
when you knew her biblically
you felt complete
and free
While I tried to hide the hole
in my chest
long enough to seek medical
attention
and
routine
close minded
open heart surgery

hoping I passed
away on the table

"How
will
I
ever survive"

the rest
of my life
I slept
with my knife
trying not to
be
the one
to attack
an innocent
out of the blinding pain of my
own strife

but at the same time
lying
in wait
for the next one
who decides
to take
love
from me
and
lay
waste
to
it
in hot beds
on cold nights

this is my post-op
recovery piece
by
peace
for the Love
of others

but
as my wounds heal
they scream
Why
did you
take your
love from
me...

and turn it
to lust
for another?

Taylor is Trouble?
describe her
And sometimes I wonder if I
want to hold her hand
Or just be close enough to
touch her
Or just be close enough

Being a femme can be so
difficult
For me it is at least
Especially when I see another
femme whose better and more
feminine than what I could
ever hope to be
Close enough

For the record
This is not going to end with a
message of empowerment
This is from a vent
connected to air ducts
That are clogged up
With the dark stuff I don't like
to mention

Taylor Swift
After a new wound
I soon started to realize
I'm always the source

The Passion of the Christ
I Love you
From the bottom of my
Bloody
Pulsing
Heart

Beatings
Pounding
Blunt force
Trauma
Ploughing
Smashing
Ran through

Fuck...
Anything?

No
Pain
But
I just won't
And I know what kills you

Though some of you were
happy to die alone
While I was
still
Impaled
Feigning
For your sake

Leave it
In
Contemplating my personal
failings
Out
of options

Yall talk too much
But don't truly have
what it takes
Life
Acting Like
You gon bring the Pain
Suffering and Death of my
Savior to me
Passion in you trying to make
me call Him

Passion in you askin
"Whose is it?"
No comment

Balled up fists
Swinging
your weak
little
weapons
And still missing the point of
all this

Who's gonna pull out
The sword from the stone
Forged with purpose
To end it

Who can kill the invincible
with a Death wish?

Prey
On that

Do Not Touch The Kittens In The Shelter

This is a public service
announcement
Kittens are cute and fuzzy
Also warm
But I must strongly advise you
not to touch, play, or cuddle
them
Unless you are choosing them

Now you may think as a little
paw stretches out and reaches
for you, "Oh there's no harm
in that" but

To be noticed
Picked up
Surveyed
Played with
And held close to the heart
Only to be gently put down
Due to some undisclosed
Reason that boils down to
The inability to care…

Could be quite painful
From the perspective of
The kind and soft kitten
In question

I can't know that for certain.
This is just what I would
imagine.

Though some may enjoy that
small glimpse of what it is to
be kept
Just to be safe
Just
Don't

Personal Jinx
You're my best kept secret
My most open humiliation
Quiet as it's kept
I haven't written for you yet
Because I won't let you go

You think it an honor to have
a poem
You think I'd adore you more
if you were a muse
No
Have you not noticed

When someone takes my
breath away, turning my blood
From red
blue
silver(like unicorns)
And slashes my heart open to
let it pour onto these pages
recreating these seemingly
magical people and places
I must be wounded to make it
so?

All of the beautiful figures I
draw with my own blood
Not only serve as testaments
of love and reverence
They are as one would hear
last words
These people live on through
my bleeding heart as pre-
written eulogies
Because I expect them to
leave without paying respects
After they've buried me
This is how I prepare

What business do you have
with such a practice?

I pray that if I remain silent
I won't die by your hand
Pushing me into a void
With no soul
No silver magic in the
blackness
To bring me back

On topic
You have not prompted me to
write
Because deep down
I am hoping that you are the
living poetry that I will never
have to keep record of
For you will be with me
presently
Always changing
Hurting
Healing
And very real

I want to hold more of you
than a few pages in my
notebook ever could.
So please
Don't make me
Make a place for you here
Don't make me
Don't

Warm Boy
I brought another person here
to die

And I'm crying because in my

madness I don't like to
remember that I was the one
to pull the trigger.

So I mourn like I lost you too

This is new for me
Still not used
to being the villian

Not used
to being the one to martyr the
innocent

In cold blood
Running through
My vainglorious pursuit
Of spoiling
Things
Rotten

No

With love still burning in the
chest
Such a hot head
And fire in the belly now

I could have sworn you were
still warm
But rigor mortis is settled in

The hard part

Made it clear that there be no
failsafe or bell for him

He requested this

Because where he's going

I don't exist.
But I did
The least I could do
show some respect and
Bury him

And hope he knows that I still
love
The way the sun hits him
Even if it's through the
ground

To Die For

I was talking to my very good
friend and life saver via text
message today.
We were discussing You.
We were discussing Love.

I confessed that the last time
that I felt crippling deep
romantic love for someone
was with the muse I met
before I'd been killed.

I pressed send
remembered him
took him apart again
to place him back in storage
almost forgetting this last

Peace...quiet
Silent like…
I could never mention Love
without it.
You know I've adored Death
ever since
I should stay focused
The piece I left out had to do
with the strength and impact
of this Love.

I have loved others.
deeply
wholeheartedly

I give unfailing Love casually
and often without good
reason.
It's nothing for me to lay
down my life when my heart is
already with Death.
What made that remembered
Love so deep
so desperate
so clingy
Possessive

Life!

Just the memory of him put
me on the fence.
I am thinking, Lord.
Do I want
Could I handle
Do I even deserve
not the Love that compels me
to give my life to Death
Could I love someone enough
to live for them?

This must be why
elderly couples die together
within days of each other
parents lose children and say
"I can't breathe"
Why they pledge, bargain,
plead to make me fear, cheat,
flee and hate Death like
humans do?

Fighting for every breath
Crying and begging the one
behind the gun NOT to shoot
your shot
and survive
To ask for more days
on this Earth
just to be with them
and alive

What a concept
You know what?
I'm just going
to grow
more confused
and upset without help
So I'll ask the people
Do you feel that
It is worth living
Who do you love more than
Death himself?

Lightning Source UK Ltd.
Milton Keynes UK
UKHW021827231219
355918UK00020B/531/P